BOA
EDITIONS
LIMITED

Postcards from the Interior

Postcards from the Interior

Wyn Cooper

BOA EDITIONS, LTD.   ROCHESTER, NY   2005

First Edition
05 06 07 08   7 6 5 4 3 2 1

Publications by BOA Editions, Ltd. — a not-for-profit corporation under
section 501 © (3) of the United States Internal Revenue Code — are made
possible with the assistance of grants from the Literature Program of the New
York State Council on the Arts; the Literature Program of the National
Endowment for the Arts; the Sonia Raiziss Giop Charitable Foundation; the
Lannan Foundation; the Mary S. Mulligan Charitable Trust; the County of
Monroe, NY; the Rochester Area Community Foundation; the Elizabeth F.
Cheney Foundation; the Ames-Amzalak Memorial Trust in memory of Henry
Ames, Semon Amzalak and Dan Amzalak; the Chadwick-Loher Foundation in
honor of Charles Simic and Ray Gonzalez; the Steeple-Jack Fund; and the CIRE
Foundation, as well as contributions from many individuals nationwide.

See Colophon on page 72 for special individual acknowledgments.

Cover Design: Steve Smock
Cover Art: Michaela Harlow
Interior Design and Composition: Scott McCarney
Manufacturing: United Graphics, Inc., Lithographers
BOA Logo: Mirko

www.wyncooper.com

Library of Congress Cataloging-in-Publication Data

Cooper, Wyn, 1957–
    Postcards from the interior / Wyn Cooper.— 1st ed.
        p. cm. — (American poets continuum series ; v. 92)
    ISBN 1-929918-65-8 (pbk. : alk. paper)
    I. Title. II. Series.

    PS3553.O628P67 2005
    811'.54—dc22

    2004028148

BOA Editions, Ltd.
Thom Ward, Editor
David Oliveiri, Chair
A. Poulin, Jr., President & Founder (1938–1996)
260 East Avenue, Rochester, NY 14604
www.boaeditions.org

NATIONAL
ENDOWMENT
FOR THE ARTS

State of the Arts

NYSCA

In memory of Penelope Austin (1951–2003)

I would like to write you so simply, so simply, so simply. Without having anything ever catch the eye, excepting yours alone, and what is more while erasing all the traits, even the most inapparent ones, the ones that mark the tone, or the belonging to a genre (the letter for example, or the post card), so that above all the language remains self-evidently secret, as if it were being invented at every step, and as if it were burning immediately, as soon as any third party would set eyes on it.

Jacques Derrida,
The Post Card: From Socrates to Freud and Beyond

CONTENTS

Postcards from Vermont

Postcards from the Interior

Postcards from Vermont

Postcard from This Place

This bird on the branch can't feel the season. It flies from
    tree to tree, north-south, north-south.
This odd little car is stuck between two trucks, which take
    it up the highway at terrible speed.
This harbor frozen over is like no harbor I know. If I can't
    see the water it must not be there.
This strange little bar is tucked between two houses, which
    keep it from going anywhere.
This message arrived today: Leave now or be sorry later. I
    don't know which to choose.
This tiny travelling circus is setting up in my field. Will
    they ask me to perform?
So far down the ladder the pickings are slim, but I know
    slim and fit in fine.
This bag full of money means nothing to me, but no you
    can't have it.
This close to the border it's best to be a bird and fly over.

Postcard from Imaginary Storms

As my eyes rise toward it the sun
glows whiter than the town it shines on.
Puddles nearly blind me as I walk
the only street: five Victorians, three
doublewides, one store and a Mobil.

The first man I see on the sidewalk
grabs my arm and won't let go,
tells me how bad winter will be.
He gives details of each imagined storm.

He loosens his grip, says the woman
he loves has treated more than one man
badly. His voice wavers, a note
held too long. He squints like me
against the sun, and from nowhere
holds his tongue.

Postcard from Green River

The church towers over the village
like a god: imagine that.
Only three of the residents are bad.
No one knows the word for loud.

Postcard from Searsburg

What was it you wanted he calls out the door
as I walk toward his house, which tilts uphill.
I just wanted to ask, I start to say—but he
cuts me off, tells me he doesn't talk to strangers,
says that I should go away. I tell him I like
his old car, I name the year and model,
and soon he is shaking my hand,
inviting me in for home-brewed beer.

After my second and his who-knows-
how-many pints, he tells me he's ready
for the government when they come.
He takes me down to the cellar, filled
with enough food for years, calendars
for the coming one, enough water for
about a month. He shows me the vegetables
he's growing under lights, but I can't see them.

I swirl out the door like the windmills
we watched from his den, ten spinning,
one broken. I stand in his driveway
and feel them, their slow whipping roar.
The town's elevation is unmatched,
except by a few of its people, higher
than kites from the slogans they write
on the outsides of their dwellings,
which no wind has managed to blow down.

Postcard from Readsboro

Where have all the people gone?
Back to 1950s West Virginia,
where the hollows are hollers
and the gardeners aren't gay.
Everyone has a hole in their exhaust,
and lets the kids spraypaint the pickups.
To keep insurance down, the bar serves
only beer in cans. Joe McCarthy
is a good man according to a drunk
who looked me up and down twice
when I came in from the cold.
Above the bar, gathering smoke,
is a 300 pound bear, stuffed
and standing almost as still
as the patrons, who wait to hear
my order, their faces a mix
of confusion and relief
when I order them back to the present.

Postcard from Whitingham

Famous polygamist Brigham Young came into the world here. He led the Mormons from Illinois to Utah, adding wives as he went, until he had 27. When he got to the valley of the Great Salt Lake, he said "This is the place," and stayed. But Vermont has not forgotten him. A hundred years ago, a local farmer took a buggy ride with his wife. When they returned, someone had placed a large stone marker 20 feet from their house, which still says today: BRIGHAM YOUNG BORN ON THIS SPOT 1801 A MAN OF MUCH COURAGE AND SUPERB EQUIPMENT.

A grand old paddleboat, combustion powered, takes tourists out on the reservoir, which winds its way a dozen miles through the mountains. A nude beach, next to a gay nude beach, neither of which are beaches but short rock cliffs that angle toward the water, are the parts of the cruise the tourists remember. The boat goes in close, the shutters click, and no one feels right about it. A few years ago the nudists got together and rented the boat, then took off their clothes when they were half a mile from the dock. They made the pilot steer the boat in close to the regular beaches, the boat put-ins, and the main road that runs along one side. Never once did any of them mention Brigham Young, emancipator of sorts, whose first house looked down on what is now a shimmering lake in the summer sun.

Postcard from Sodom

The only clue to where it was, except a few stone foundations, is the small green sign for someone's driveway and the lush summer path beyond: Sodom Road, Private, Dead End. It goes up from Moss Hollow. It's where Marlboro meets Halifax, and look what happened.

The stories of its name vary with the people who tell them, though they all concern pleasure. What varies most is the degree of approval. The shapes their mouths make when they speak, the way they use their hands, the words they choose: proof they're telling the same story.

Vermonters are known for leaving each other to do as they please, but some say the Sodomites were driven out for their behavior. Others insist their overindulgence caused their demise, or they would be here still. The final theory, painfully boring, concerns weather patterns and overfarming.

Hard to believe corn once grew here. The trees are thick and tall, the terrain all hills and gullies. Maybe they tried to make life easy. Cows were for steak instead of milk. Sunrise meant time to go to bed, to fall where they stood beside their stills. And maybe it's nobody's business.

Postcard from Halifax

If you turn left out of our driveway, the road follows the Green River, a hundred feet below. If you hike the steep hill down to the water you'll notice the pools the river makes. When I bought this house, a carpenter told me that if I was lucky, and went down to the river on a hot August day, I might see a couple of hippy girls skinny dipping. It was clear to him this was the best thing about the house.

When the road turns to dirt you're in Guilford, but if you take the first left you'll come back in a different way, up Hale Road past my friend Molly's house, who can sing like Nina Simone in 23 languages but makes her living as a healer. She also leads a church choir. Of all the psychics she knows, and she knows quite a few, the woman whose vision she most believes says Halifax is the spiritual center of the universe.

The next mile has its own things to say about statements like that. Six feet from the roadside a monument tall as a child bends at an angle that makes your neck sore to read: IN MEMORY OF JOHN BOLSTER THROWN FROM HIS HORSE NEAR THIS PLACE 1810 AGED 80. The small house on whose lawn the monument sits has three birdhouses mounted on tall sticks, and a woodpile a hundred feet long.

Two summers ago 30 people on horses crossed the road here, to get to the next trail. One of them was a man from Providence, Rhode Island. He had been a mounted policeman there for 27 years. Something happened with the horse, one he had never ridden. He was in the air, then on the ground as the horse ran away. The hysterical riders used Molly's phone to call for help, but it was too late.

After you cross two one-lane bridges the llamas appear, running beside an electric fence. Behind this farm, Spirit Hill, off a barely worn trail—you're walking now—beside a fallen oak, is another monument, cemented to an oval rock: HIS WIFE KATHERINE E. NICHOLS MURDERED NEAR THIS PLACE OCTOBER 9, 1913. The first time I found it, and for more than a year after, there was a water bottle tied around the stone.

Follow the bog north to the old foundation, take a right, and find the stone for Elizabeth's husband. The only difference is that it says KILLED AT THIS SPOT. The man who shot them worked in their apple orchard, and was said to have had a crush on her. After they were dead, he tied a string to his rifle's trigger and shot himself. When my former neighbor Brian found the first stone, it was October 9, 1993, 80 years to the day.

The orchard is gone, and Brian has moved to New York. The wildflowers still appear in late April, the trees still grow thick with leaves, and the animals come out of hiding to wander these woods: moose, deer, bear, fox, and the occasional coydog, whose bark can be heard above the chainsaws of those who want the trees in their woodpile, or to use for floors and counters in the houses they make in the clearings and call home.

Postcard from Glastonbury

In the first five years after World War Two, 11 hikers disappeared inside these town lines. Those who live nearby barely get out of their cars. Not that there's much to do, except look at the woods, and there's no one to see—64 square miles, and not a single resident. When I explore the long-abandoned roads, they follow a path that has nothing to do with the land they traverse. They seem to be spelling something I can't read, no matter how many times I retrace my route. I think it might be two long words.

Postcard from The Man of Kent

At Richard's parents' house on Terrible Mountain, looking down toward the pond, I shot my first and only gun. It had been in his family a hundred years, made during the Civil War, and was so loud my ears still ring. The week before, I took him to The Man of Kent, a pub just over the border, run by a man from Kent named John, a friend of mine. Richard suddenly found it amusing to tease John about England losing the Revolutionary War. If I had seen it coming I would have tried to stop it, but soon John was seething. We almost had to leave, but some bikers pulled in, and John knew which English ale each one wanted. Richard apologized—I blamed it on the gun—and John led us in a toast to the Queen.

Postcard from Robert Frost's Grave

Amy was crooning and Linda was swooning the night I brought them here. Her baritone led us in Irish songs of mourning, liquid as the Guinness which helped us sing. Linda asked that we show respect, but the director relieved himself behind two birches that grow near the grave. We were louder than fireworks on the Fourth of July, which we watched from the End of the World. We sang along with Amy as Linda rubbed the stone. The northern lights lit up our thoughts, but cops arrived to shut us up. A lover's quarrel with the world indeed.

Postcard from Halifax Gorge

Four friends and I made our way down
the cliffs to the lowest pool, below the last
waterfall, where three men fished in silence.
We descended in sneakers, towels over
our shoulders. When we reached the water
they pulled in their lines and left without
a word to each other or to us, escapees
fishing for dinner just off the main road.

Postcard from Harmony Parking Lot

The teens have gathered, because they are teens.
They wear brown shirts faded to beige, black
boots, low-slung jeans. The way they stand
is called jaunty. Cigarettes burn through
their words, smoke blows through their hair,
and the way they stare at passersby blends
reptile with bird, spleen with wonder,
your past with their present to you.

Postcard from Westminster West

The fields are greener than the wildest future,
each turn a new vista of sheep and sky,
the day as bright as the impulse to drive here.
I can't believe you brought me to Scotland,
she says. We've never been there,
but know it must look like this.
The road winds downhill to the river,
green as the summer grass, no boats
to disturb its slow way south.
We drive home on a freeway free of cars,
91 south to Brattleboro, looking down
on rivers that join together, one wild,
one calm, one taking the name of the other.

Postcard from Guilford

In this square pasture expensive horses run in circles. Their compass moves clockwise inside the fence, orbits of the time of year. It's spring. The mares kick mud as they run, slip but don't fall, intent on the rings they create. Their owner catches me unaware. Her look tells me she doesn't want to talk about the horses, so I ask if she thinks it will snow again. She pushes some mud around with her boot, then tells me the horses do this the first day of April, every year. She says it is common. They're not chasing each other, she goes on, though it may look that way. Something tells me her story is false. I try to look in the horses' eyes, to see if I can find the truth. I remember the date and reach into my pocket, here at my own expense.

Postcard from Wethersfield

What we don't know hurts us,
we know that much. Our inability
to discuss quantum mechanics
makes conversation meaningless,
makes washing the dishes take us
to the edge of despair. The capital
of a country we've never heard of
is nowhere near the tips of our tongues,
which wag instead at the weather.
What language do they speak there?
Do they wonder like us if it will rain?

Postcard of Saxton's River, 1910

Five men strike five poses in front of the general store. In the middle distance, the snow is as tall as the woman who walks toward them. The men wear coats of their own sheep's wool, befitting the season but not the day. They sweat beneath their hats. The woman thought it warmer than it was, and chose a thin dress, which according to the men was just right. Three of them look as if they'd just been caught watching her strut. One looks straight ahead, his hands in his lap. The final man, closest to the camera, his face open to the moment's movement, smiles broadly at the woman walking, it appears, his way.

Postcard from the Wind

In fall the wind blows cold one night,
then stays that way for half the year.
I fly inside from wall to wall.

Each bird to its tree, says the wind,
each bug to its leaf, each trace
of lipstick blown away.

Postcard from a Late Nor'easter

What greater pleasure than this, to sit
outside in late April, in Vermont,
and watch the snow blow in from Boston.

It whirls around the daffodils, yellow
until they fold themselves into white.
It means nothing this time of year.

The wind carries other things, stories
of witches burned for their ways,
men of the cloth who deserve the same.

The snow stops and everything's still,
your breath, my breath, the grass
working hard to be green under white.

Postcard from Fishing Season

Not the land so much as who lives here now.
Not the way that man stares me up and down—
just what is he trolling for, exactly?
Not the mud into which my car sinks
on the road that follows the river
I live on, the one fishermen love
for its lack of fish, the better to sip beer,
tell stories that exist for just this reason,
the subject of fact and speculation,
what makes us try to catch them.

Postcard from the Rain

August and the river looks like April,
high as my chest and moving fast,
green as the leaves it runs underneath.
I follow its lazy curve to the dam,
where it falls hard to the pool below
in waves, in waves, a pulse.

A family of eight lives further down
who only eat what they can grow,
which this year's rain has killed.
They're selling furniture on the lawn,
chairs cobbled together with glue,
lamps that don't work for a dollar.
I give them corn I bought at the store,
not sweet like what they grew last year.

Postcard from Before TV

Now that I'm here I stand straighter, shoulders
back where they belong, feet finding
their way over uneven terrain, eyes
keen to see everything—birds
in bushes along the river, which roars
in late summer, dog days we didn't
get last month, dogs pursuing leaves
red in mid-September, firewood handily
gathered already. Now these flames keep
me warm, what they watched before TV.

Postcard Recipe from Hunting Season

Gunshots turn me sideways in my chair,
face me out the window, duck sitting
pretty for the kill. But it's not me
they want, they want the hearts of deer
in their sights, slung in the backs of their
pickups for show. Then they want them
cooked in a pan over uneven heat,
in Sprite instead of wine, ketchup
instead of butter. Kill what is legal,
I say, but don't cook it badly.

Postcard from November

Night barely has a chance
to erase the day and you
have to mention it, how
little light there is, late
November of the number
of years since Jesus was born,
someone we don't believe in
but still count our years by.
We assume he forgives us,
and anyone else who misses
the point. The night is starry,
the planets glow with effect.
Tiny clouds are pushed in
circles by a breeze we wish
more brisk, something to blow
this hallowed weather away.

Postcard to a Secret Address

I have the address at which no one else writes you,
far up the mountain where you go to stay cool.
Are you still as strange as when we courted?
I write you wherever I am.

What brought me so far up river no one
can figure. The locals try to make me talk—
fill me with beer, slap my back, tell me
I've come all this way for nothing
when what they mean is welcome home.

Postcard Advice

Wander these woods with your pants
tucked into high leather boots—
snakes have been reported.
Take a southwesterly course
until you smell a proper meal.
Try not to be early or late,
and don't forget to bring dessert.

Make conversation move quickly
from topic to gossip to joke.
Try not to look at their clothes,
in every way unlike your own.
Don't be surprised when they pick
at their dinners. They're saving
room for what you brought.

Postcards from the Interior

Postcard from the Bus

Notorious humbug, unlovely rider of buses
everywhere, tell me you remember the night
we met between Flint and Detroit, and I'll
tell you exactly what you taught me: not
to believe in the lives of saints, the death
of God or the genius of the insane, but
to watch the moving dark for the lights
of the next town, the one that's half-
way there, halfway not, painfully
close to the one I forgot.

Postcard from Hell

I'm less than an hour northwest of Ann Arbor, on the second-most winding road in Michigan. Hell is perched on a hill above a man-made lake, 40 or so houses, a few stores, and Damn Creek, which runs under the intersection. Postcards in the store say Greetings from Hell, Welcome to Hell, Go to Hell. The guy pumping my gas tells me about the weathermen on the Detroit TV stations, how they try not to laugh when they report every November that Hell froze over last night. I am cold without you, not burning in hell like I thought I would be.

Postcard from a Dream

Not even the northern star could tell us where we are.
The No Trespassing sign is not in a language we know.

We walk past it, into this forest that won't return us
the same. New sounds grow louder as night comes on.

We feel where water springs from the ground,
follow it down the mountain to an oval lake.

Everyone is awake when we arrive, floating on houseboats
lit by candles, whistling like birds after rain.

Postcard from the Flight

She sits next to me on the jet
to London, hair a tumble of curl
and shine, lap full of treats
for the trip. I am in love
before she says hello.

A gambler would bet everything
on a horse the color of her hair,
which falls briefly on my shoulder,
and I would bet the same
it won't fall there again.

Postcard from Copenhagen

In Hans Christian Andersen's house
the light is blue, the climate dense.
A thin vapor floats on the surface
of every last word and glance.
A narrow sidewalk circumscribes
two sides of the building, a corner
of cobblestone streets no one
stops to smoke on anymore.

In Hans Christian Andersen's house
no one can stay for long.
The roof's too steep to climb
except by beast, the chimney
a crumbling twenty foot spire.
No one understands desire,
how it can make you skate away
in winter and not come back.

Postcard from Le Chateau de Picasso

He's buried here, but no one is allowed in.
I stole onto the grounds the back way, down
Mont Saint Victoire. The chateau, too big
to call home, 500 years old,
rises above a forest of scrub trees.

All four corners, two of which face
down the canyon to Aix-en-Provence,
are turrets that combine the sexes,
cylindrical towers capped with sun-seeking
breasts, as if drawn by the former owner.

Postcard from Capri

It rises straight up from the sea,
as high as it is wide.

Cliffs drop like rain
they haven't had in months.

I hear the cries
of nymphs and satyrs.

White rocks bake in the sun.
I have left something undone.

Postcard in a Bottle

I'm far from anything I know,
tired and cold, sailing with
strange men on dark water.
I have news of the enemy
but no one will listen.
I come up with a plan
to trick them into hearing
what they need to know.
I've spent a week playing it
out in my head. It involves
a cork, holy water, voodoo,
but even that is telling too much.

Stellar Ray Postcard

The martinet is in the minaret, not the other way around.
He summons us to nightly prayer and not, we hope, its
opposite. Stellar rays are on the mosque, which floats in the
night like a barge. The voices rise as one until they reach a
certain pitch, which wavers in the air like bees. We don't
join in, and no one cares, as lost in what they believe as we
are lost in what we don't. When the prayers are done the
faithful stamp their way home, as if they don't expect an
answer. The dust they raise shines against the stone walls,
lustrous beacons in the dark.

Postcard from My Post

Neither day nor dollar goes by
this room I watch from,
locked in from outside
for almost a season.

They tell me I left my post,
what I guarded a mystery,
a history of desertion
in my family tree.

They say lots of things
they ought not to,
as if to prove a point
no one can rue.

Postcard from the Canon

The long strong arm of a law
  we thought to be off the books
    holds us so still we feel the planet
      spin through space as we lip-sync
        grace before another vainglorious meal.

        Less than our space is taken for granted
      by powers judged higher than ours
    who attempt to prevail in covert
  and offhand ways but manage only
to bungle their first three tries.

The law dissembles despite objections
  as word becomes deed and facts are hidden
    behind mahogany from Honduras
      in a club where it is forbidden
        to own wallpaper of floral design.

        Which would spell the end to this way
      of living though no one is missing.
    The Man of La Mancha walks onto a screen
  in this very room to demonstrate
how to speak off the cuff.

We tell him in his own strange tongue
  that we have seen his face in the frame
    how it deflects what we call pain
      and why does he bother with acting
        when he has this other life.

        The plates by now are nearly empty.
      The glasses have been drunk dry.
    Blue smoke hovers over the things
  we say. We try not to disturb it
so it won't float away.

Postcard from Babel

Morning light comes sideways
through the blue glazed window.
No one moves a muscle.
Motionless birds do not sing,
but strike a songlike pose.

Later, dogs run themselves
ragged in ever smaller circles.
The only words anyone hears
are spoken from a tower
in a tongue no one knows.

Postcard from Metal

The music is meant to give nothing
but pain, it starts in the head,
goes all the way down to the feet
and back up, a screaming headache
that says less about the fans
than about the band, their souls
tossed from flame to flame,
torches that burn in their eyes.

They cause pain so others might
understand theirs, they carry
their message from city to city,
sleep with women more lovely
than their music is ugly, a lack
of meaning so complete it hurts.

Postcard Lost at Sea

He tells me everything is his now,
the island, the wind that rocks
the wreckage that once was his craft.

The blotches on his face suggest
sun or regret. The word
he hates most is *accident*.

I hang on to each thread
of his fabrication, a yarn
he wraps around himself.

He had to have power somewhere,
and to get here came by boat
to see if he could leave a wake.

He looks at my clothes and sees a sail.
I tell him I have been here longer.
My words billow in the wind of his eyes.

Postcard from the Treetops

Every time a breeze comes up
I almost lose my grip,
I sway with the tree
no one can see
because I have walked miles
to find this slender oak.

This isn't paradise after all,
no one said it was but me
and I was wrong, short
in the brain but long
on the limb from which
I hang, my courage
gone with the wind.

Postcard for a Painting

Send me your last painting
and I will send a postcard
in which I attack no one.

I must be losing my angry
young man silhouette,
slipping into a gauzy
side-view of the boundless
nada of the new millennium.

There's news from the front,
where I fight, and from
the back, where I run
when I can't take any more.

Postcard from a Rocket

This rocket I'm riding has power
to tear down the walls of prayer.
It follows the curve of the earth,
it measures its length and girth.

This tunnel I'm digging is long
but the light at the end is wrong.
It shows me something I've seen,
a place crazy with green.

This rocket flies me almost home.
It lands instead outside the known,
where mountains are shaped like saddles,
the flanks below scarred by battles.

Postcard from What I Think

I think the sun is a made-up
thing lit entirely by Russians
who move its image like clockwork
across the sky we watch daily
for signs of foreign invasion.

I think the god who made us
has gone on to better things
made of nitrous and honey
which no money can buy.

I think Seven Brides for
Seven Brothers is the best
film ever made in color,
red is fastest for cars,
that if you don't stop
staring I'll call the cops.

Postcard from a Feast

It's all in your mind they tell me,
but I can't find it there—does it hide
behind nightmares, too shy to speak?
Does it wander the alleys looking
for just the right trash, does it follow
me home and tell me how to act?

I don't know what to make of this feast
laid out in my honor, the beige
and the brown, the blue and the grey,
colors I never thought of as savory
until my mouth began to water today.

Postcard to You

It's from a woman who knows your real address. On the front, a photo of a lake that could be anywhere, hills rising around it. On the back she tries to tell you what it's like to be her, right now, wherever she is. The stamp she licked stares you in the face as her perfume finds your nose. Maybe it drifted in the heat down her wrist onto fingers that held the pen that wrote these words. And because it had time to sink into her skin, you could swear she just floated in.

Postcard from Desire

She rides in tall on her white mare, the woman with land in her name. Her cheeks are red from the wind, her scarf lies loose on her shoulder. When I approach, I smell her hair from ten feet away—flowers, grass, perfume. She dismounts to a stance that makes me step back. Another man would follow her anywhere.

Postcard from a Wedding We Won't be Attending

Not their cars on the streets of this village,
not the evergreen hedge to make us think twice.
Not the invitation received by registered mail,
not the curtains hung lightly for such an occasion.

Not the smoked trout laid out like a corpse,
not this man, not this woman, none of their friends.
Not this time, not the next, not ever as far as we know.
And not the road we walk on, gravel uneven below.

Postcard from the Interior

A mess beyond what I thought possible,
this crooked house I found while hiking:
couches buried by papers and magazines,
tables sinking under knick-knacks,
chairs covered with clothes from decades ago,
whole rooms lost to boxes and bags.
Somehow the wallpaper matches it all,
yellow-brown, dust-grey, content
turning to form from floor to ceiling,
a sight to behold on this bright spring day.

Postcard from Independence

On this very dry Fourth of July, nothing is knee-high
except to the grasshoppers, going out of their little minds,
sending messages of love all around, but no one listens,
no one believes, no one hears them above the explosions.

Postcard from the Second Person

The world around you whirled away
by agents of dizziness, hump
in the road that fools you, cop
down the hill hiding between
the apple orchard and the bright
field of corn. He and his army
advancing, in oh! those uniforms.

The world can be painful, or dull,
it can lull you into thinking
you know what you don't.
You want to see it brow to brow,
but today the wind blows hard.

When the dust finally settles
you're home mending fences
to protect the peaches you give
to women whose names rhyme
with *fauna*, *quill*, *lavender*, and *fizz*.

Postcard from the Party

You have to be invited, and there's nothing
you can do to be asked. Headlines and bloodlines
don't help. It's a long way from home but I'm
here, the view much better than I'm used to.
How did this happen? Dumb but good luck,
right place and time, the planets aligned.
No contract, no deadline, no risk. And what
did I do to deserve this? Slept with all
the wrong people, gambled too much on friends
of friends with light bulbs over their heads.
Wrote every day no matter what.

ACKNOWLEDGMENTS

Grateful acknowledgment is made to the editors of the following magazines and anthologies, in which these poems, often in different form, first appeared:

Antioch Review: "Postcard from a Wedding We Won't Be Attending"
The Breath of Parted Lips II: Poems from The Frost Place: "Postcard from Harmony Parking Lot," "Postcard from This Place"
Crazyhorse: "Postcard from a Dream," "Postcard from an Imaginary Storm," "Postcard from the Second Person"
Denver Quarterly: "Postcard from Desire," "Stellar Ray Postcard"
Frank (France): "Postcard from Le Chateau de Picasso," "Postcard from Saxton's River, 1910"
The Journal: "Postcard from Copenhagen"
Marlboro Review: "Postcard from Fishing Season"
Northern Woodlands: "Postcard from the Interior"
Orion: "Postcard from Westminster West"
Poetry: "Postcard from the Bus," "Postcard from the Party," "Postcard from Searsburg"
Quarterly West: "Postcard from Robert Frost's Grave," "Postcard to You"
Rivendell: "Postcard from Glastonbury"
Snake Nation Review: "Postcard from the Flight," "Postcard Lost at Sea," "Postcard from November"
West Branch: "Postcard from Halifax," "Postcard from The Man of Kent," "Postcard from Readsboro," "Postcard to a Secret Address," "Postcard from Sodom," "Postcard from Wethersfield," "Postcard from Whitingham"

"Postcard from a Dream" also appeared in *In Posse* (www.webdelsol.com).
"Postcard from Glastonbury" also appeared in *Vermont Magazine*.
"Postcard to a Secret Address" and "Postcard from the Beginning" also appeared in *Poems from the Mountains*.

Sixteen of these poems were collected in *Secret Address*, a chapbook published by Chapiteau Press in 2002, with photos by Eric Slayton (www.chapiteau.org).

Six of these poems have been set to music by Madison Smartt Bell, for a CD to be released in 2006 by Gaff Music (www.gaffmusic.com).

"Postcard from Harmony Parking Lot" was read on The Writer's Almanac, May 1, 2003.

THANKS

The author wishes to thank Josh Harmon for the theory, Shawna Parker for the practice, Madison Bell for the music, Scott Beal and Don Dixon for keeping the faith, Michael Prince for Derrida, Laure-Anne Bosselaar and Kurt Brown for Vauvenargues, Anthony Hauck and Joe Mueller for their support, and all the editors who published these poems, especially Jim Schley and Ann Aspell at Chapiteau Press, Christian Wiman, Bin Ramke, Kathy Fagan, Marty Williams, Ellen Dudley, Syd Lea, Sebastian Matthews, and everyone at *Crazyhorse*, *West Branch*, and BOA Editions.

Special thanks to Michaela Harlow, friend and neighbor, for use of the cover painting, *Rain in Truro*, from her series of postcard paintings (www.michaelaharlow.com).

And an oversized postcard of thanks to Thom Ward, who saw to the heart of this book.

ABOUT THE AUTHOR

Wyn Cooper has published two previous books of poems, *The Country of Here Below* (Ahsahta Press, 1987), and *The Way Back* (White Pine Press, 2000), as well as a chapbook, *Secret Address* (Chapiteau Press, 2002). His poems, stories, essays, and reviews have appeared in *Poetry, Ploughshares, Crazyhorse, AGNI, Verse, Fence, Antioch Review*, and more than 60 other magazines. His poems are included in 20 anthologies of contemporary poetry, including *The Mercury Reader, Outsiders*, and *Ecstatic Occasions, Expedient Forms*.

In 1993, a poem from his first book, "Fun," was turned into Sheryl Crow's Grammy-winning song "All I Wanna Do." He has also cowritten songs with David Broza, David Baerwald, and Bill Bottrell. In 2003, Gaff Music released *Forty Words for Fear*, a CD of songs based on poems and lyrics by Cooper, set to music and sung by the novelist Madison Smartt Bell. It has been featured on NPR's Weekend Edition and World Café, and has been written about in *Esquire, The New York Times Magazine, The New York Observer*, and elsewhere.

Cooper has taught at the University of Utah, Bennington College, Marlboro College, and at The Frost Place, where he now serves on the advisory board. He is a former editor of *Quarterly West*, and the recipient of a fellowship from the Ucross Foundation. He lives in Halifax, Vermont, and helps organize the Brattleboro Literary Festival.

For more information on Wyn Cooper see www.wyncooper.com.

COLOPHON

Postcards from the Interior by Wyn Cooper was set in Minion and Antique Typewriter by Scott McCarney, Rochester, New York. The cover design was by Steve Smock. The cover art, *Rain in Truro* by Michaela Harlow, is courtesy of the artist. Manufacturing was by United Graphics, Inc., Lithographers.

The publication of this book was made possible in part by the special support of the following individuals:

John & Lisa Anderson

Anonymous

Scott Browning

Alan & Nancy Cameros

Burch & Louise Craig

The Draytons

Suzanne & Peter Durant

Cathy M. Ferguson

Richard & Suressa Forbes

Dr. Henry & Beverly French

Dane & Judy Gordon

Kip & Deb Hale

Peter & Robin Hursh

Robert & Willy Hursh

Meg Kearney

Archie & Pat Kutz

Rosemary & Lewis Lloyd

Robert & Francie Marx

Boo Poulin

Deborah Ronnen

Paul & Andrea Rubery

George & Bonnie Wallace

Lee & Rob Ward

Thomas R. Ward

Pat & Michael Wilder